I Have Shapes

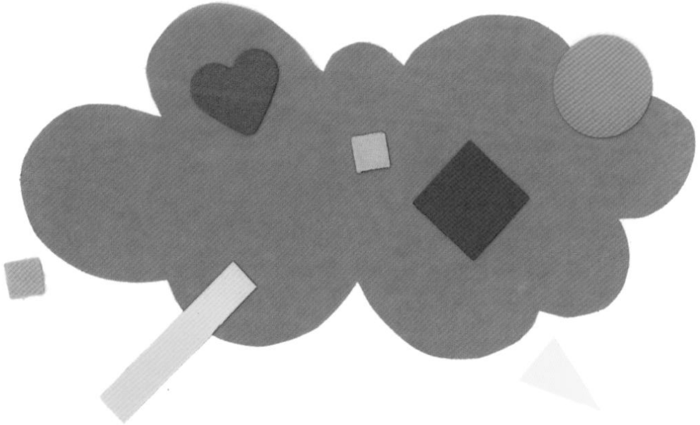

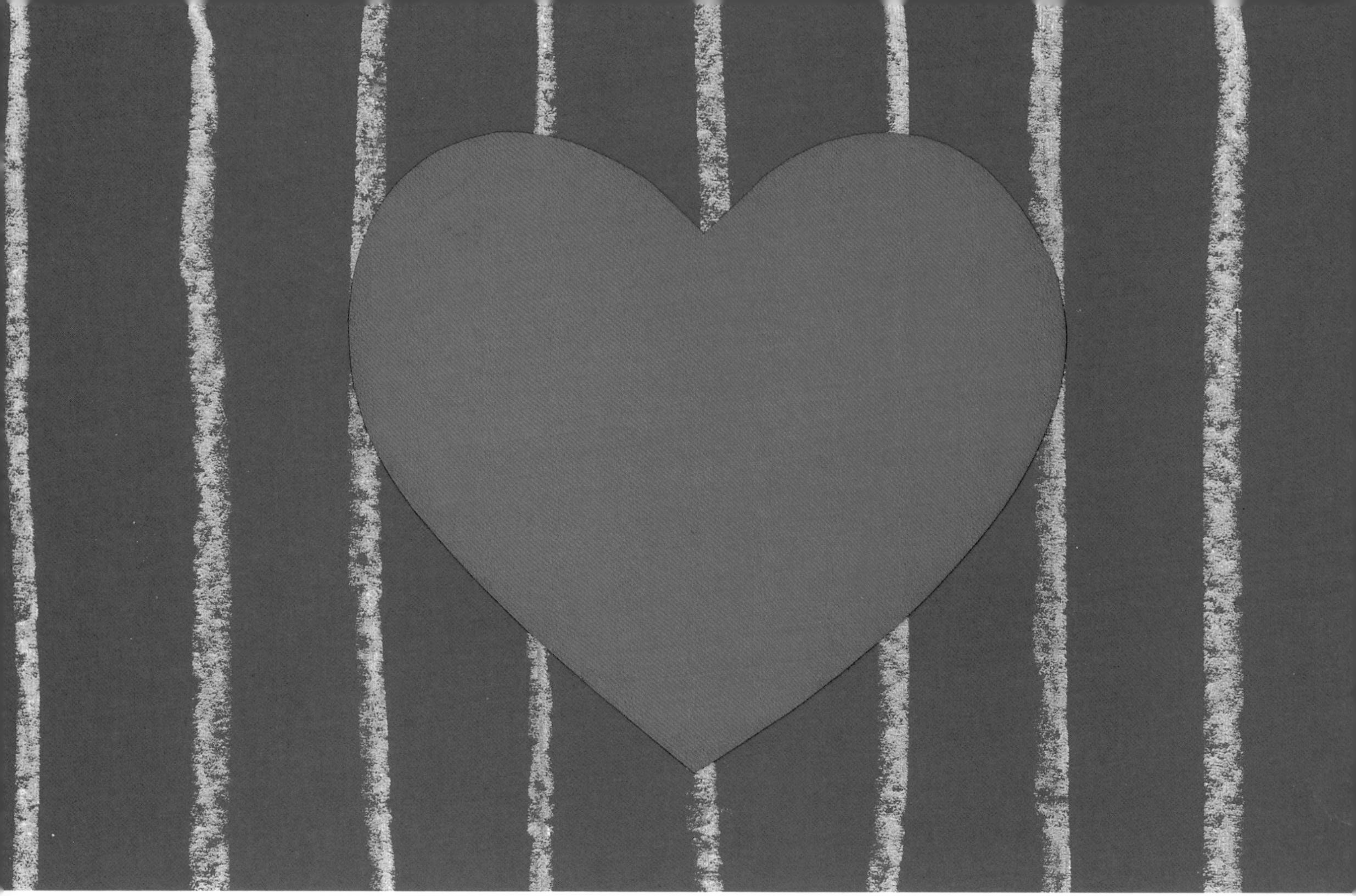

2

I have 1 heart.

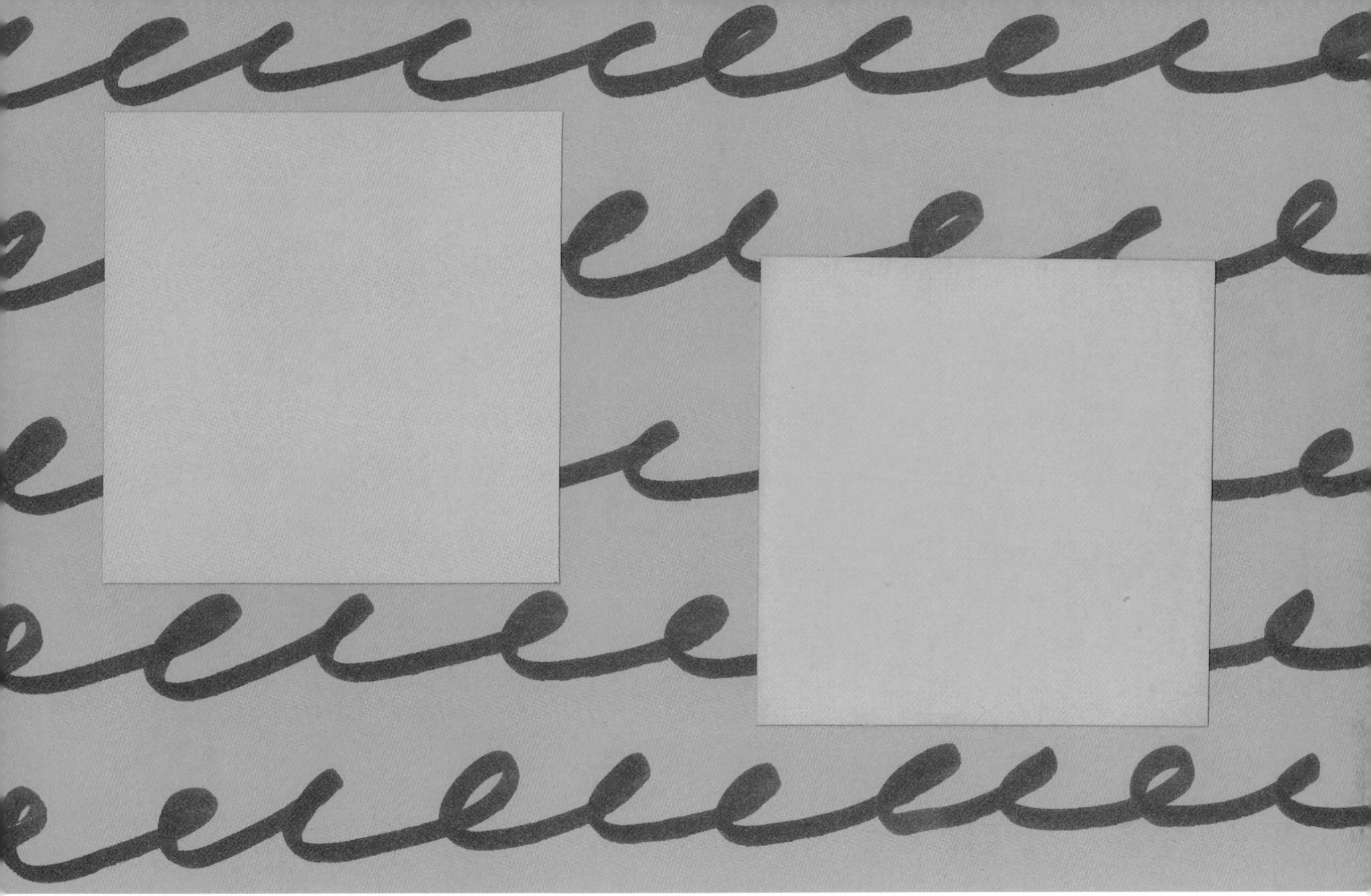

I have **2** squares.

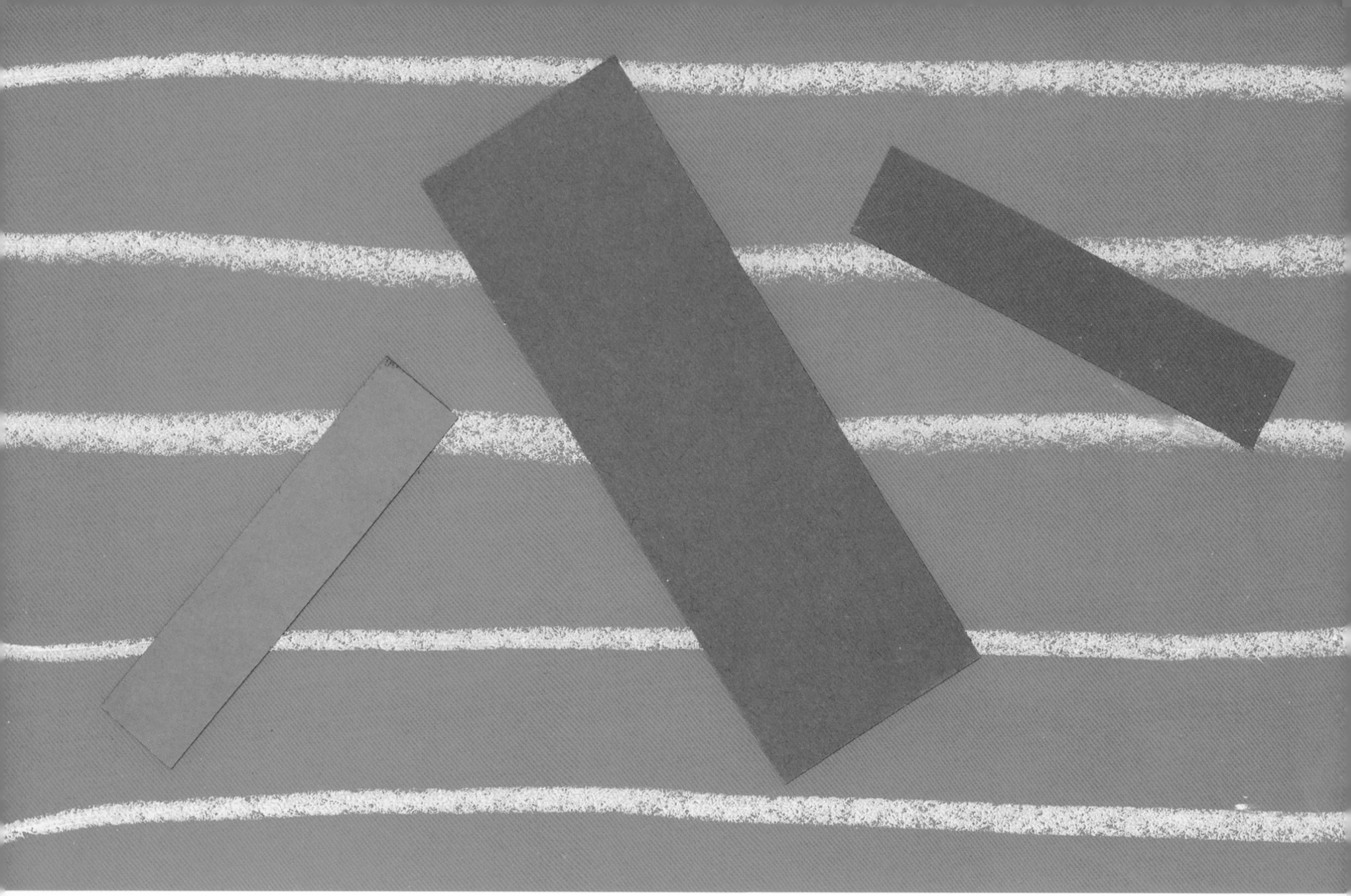

I have **3** rectangles.

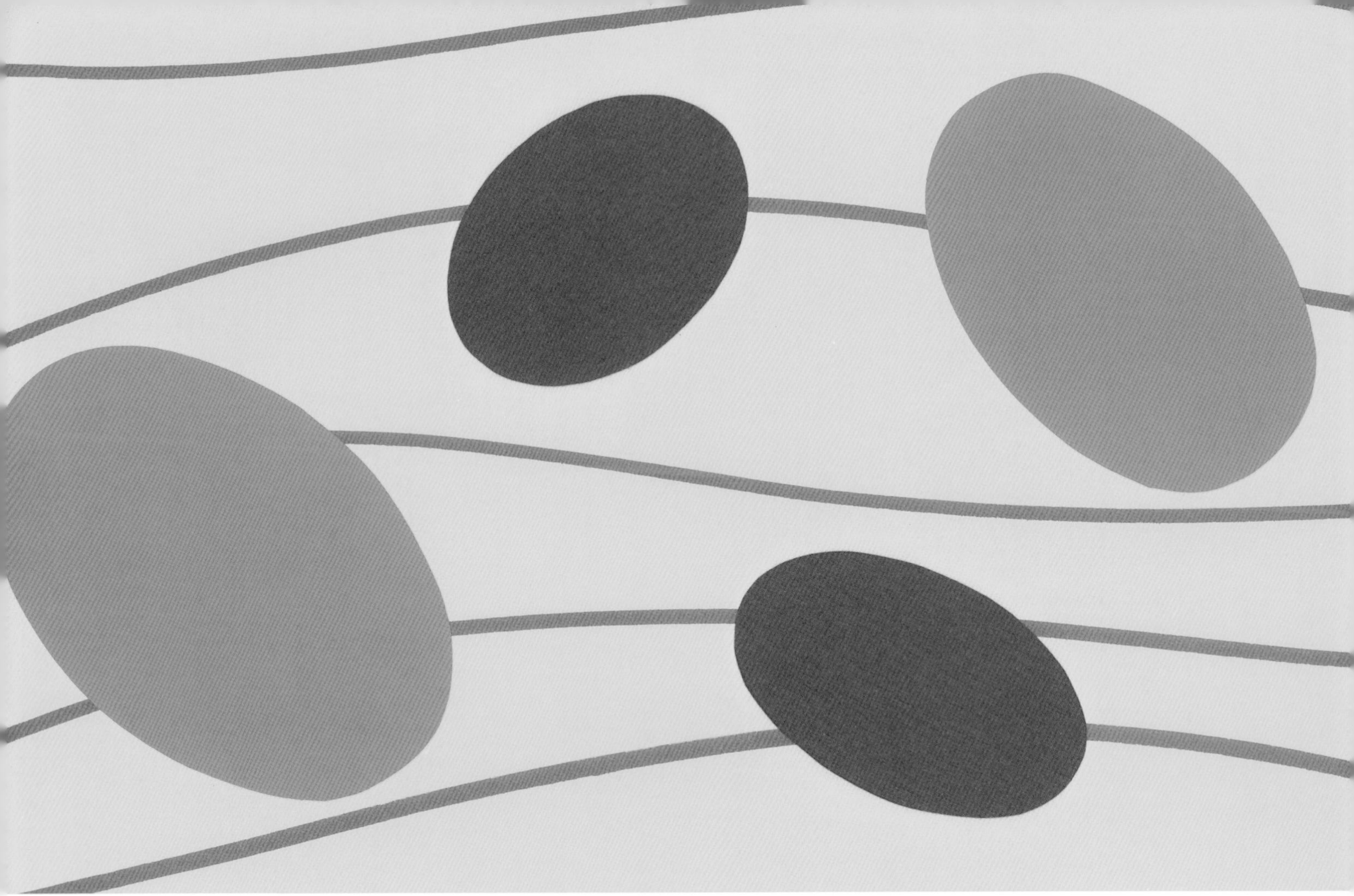

I have **4** ovals.

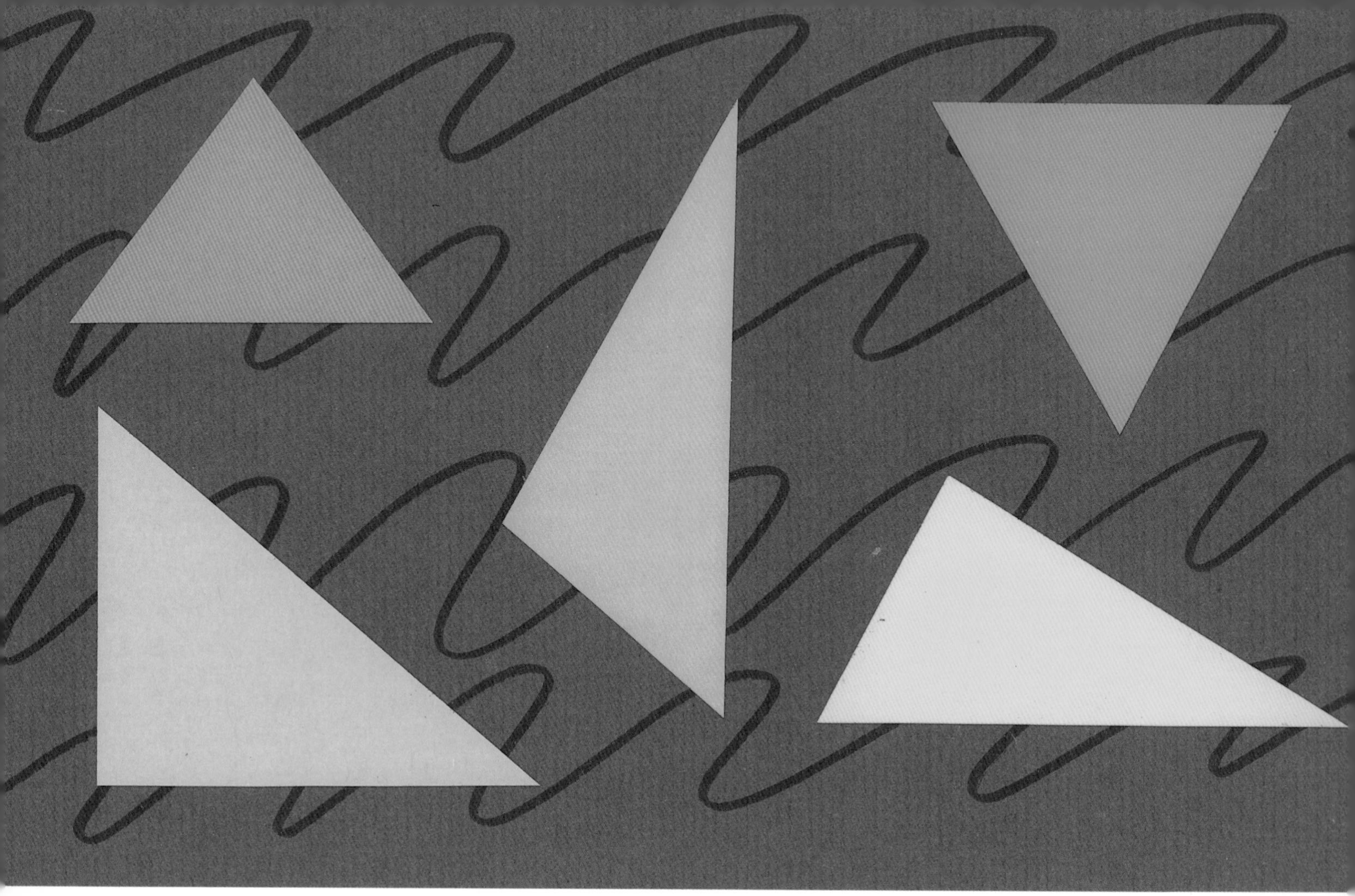

I have **5** triangles.

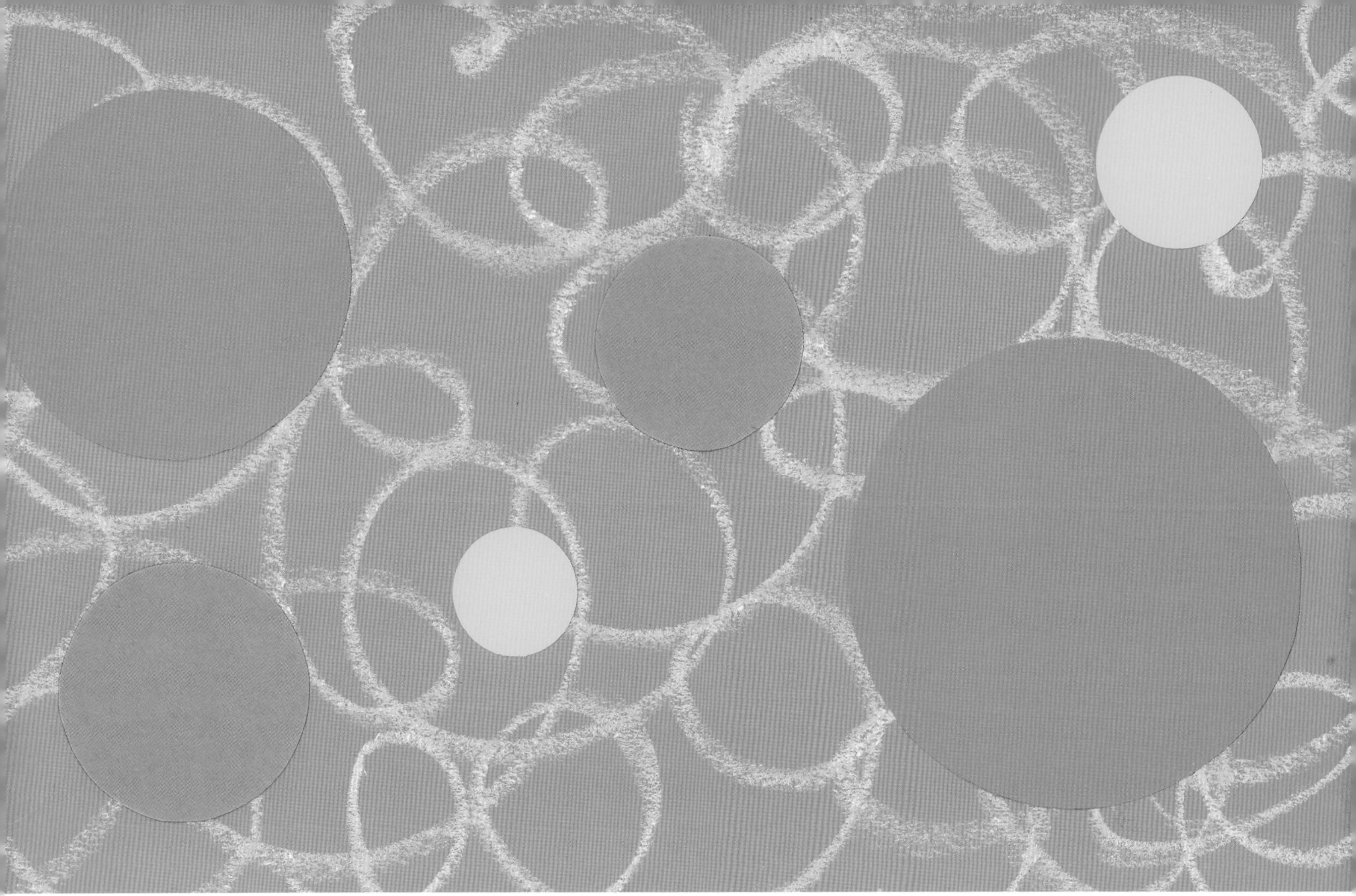

I have **6** circles.

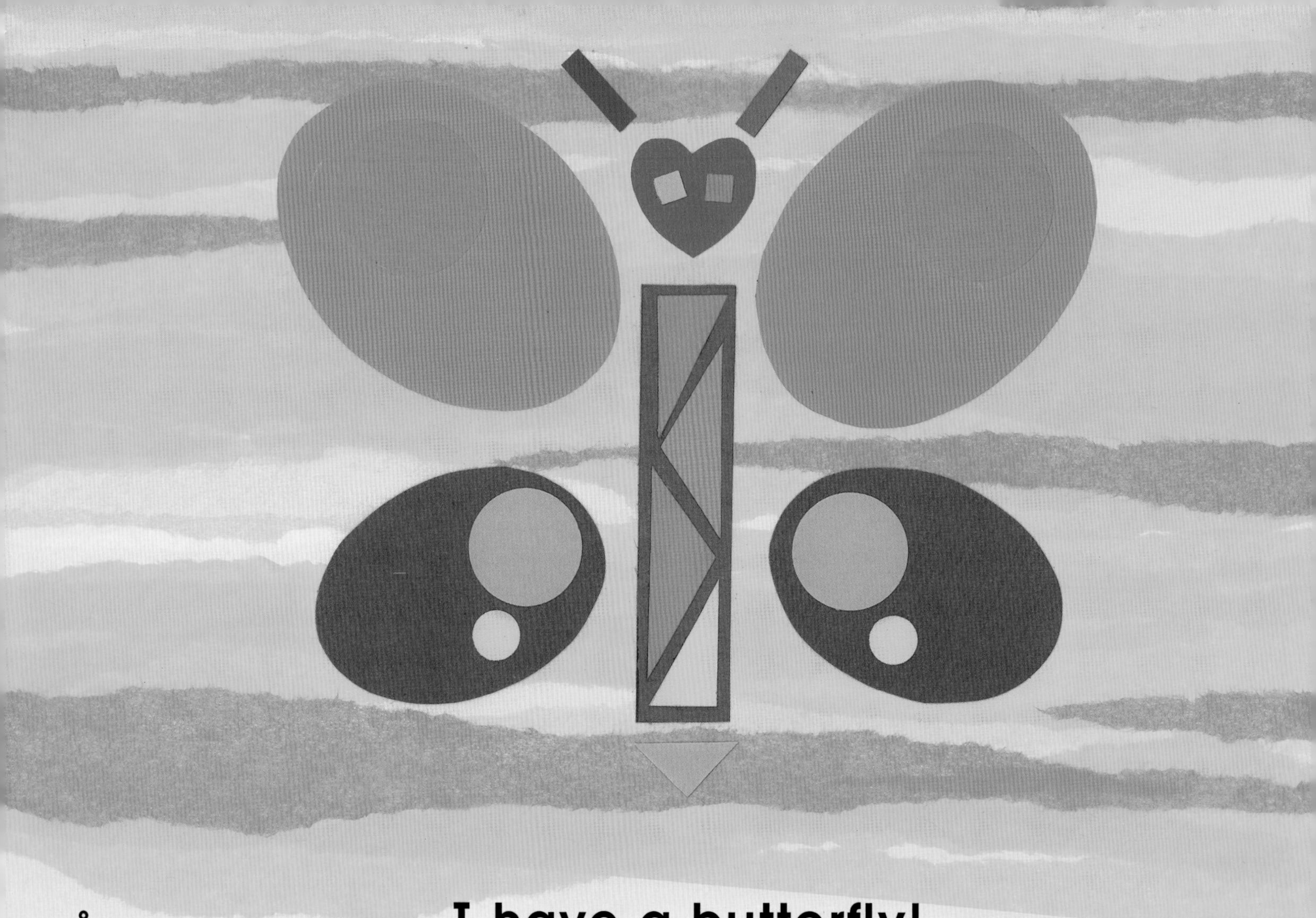

I have a butterfly!